Ms. Loops presents...

Handwriting Clues Club Books

Book 1
Clues to Find in Cursive & Print

Book 2
A-Z Dictionary of Clues

Book 3
A-Z Clues of Iggy... as found by Peony

Join the Handwriting Clues Club of
adventurous people who become clues finders!

Ms. Loops Presents...
Handwriting Clues Club – Book 3

A-Z Clues of Iggy...
as found by Peony

by Judy Kaplan
(aka Ms. Loops)

Drawings by Wayne Ramirez

Drawing of Ms. Loops by Wayne Ramirez.

Printed by KDP - https://kdp.amazon.com
ISBN: 978-1-957373-06-5 (Paperback)
ISBN: 978-1-957373-08-9 (Mobi)

Printed by Ingram Sparks - https://www.ingramspark.com
ISBN: 978-1-957373-11-9 (Hardback)
ISBN: 978-1-957373-07-2 (Epub)

Library Catalog Dewey Classification # - 155.2'82
Kaplan, Judy.
1. Graphology   2. Writing   3. Handwriting Analysis
I. Title.   II. Series.   III. Wayne Ramirez, illustrator

Judy Kaplan Books

JudyKaplanBooks.com

Acknowledgements

Thank you to the highly knowledgeable and professional handwriting analysts at these organizations:
American Handwriting Association Foundation
ahafhandwriting.org
American Association of Handwriting Analysts
aahahandwriting.org
International Grapho-Analysis Association
igas.com
Your courses, workshops, certification programs, and mentoring have been a thorough and enlightening education in handwriting analysis.

Thank you Linda Larson for your remarkably detailed evaluation of the information in this book.

Thank you to my family and friends for their incredible support, encouragement and patience throughout my writing.

Thank you to Wayne Ramirez for his wonderful depictions of my characters Ms. Loops, Iggy & Peony.

Author Information

Judy Kaplan has held a life-long fascination for writing, handwriting, and books. After a 27 year career as a High School Library Media Specialist, she began a second career as a Handwriting Analyst. She has Handwriting Analyst Certifications from both ahafhandwriting.org and igas.com. She specializes in personality and compatibility profiles. She created the Handwriting Clues Club series of books to promote understanding and compatibility in an easy, fun, and informative format for all ages.

GLOSSARY
(to refer to if wanted)

Graphology - The study of analyzing meanings in handwriting, also called Handwriting Analysis. People who analyze handwriting are called Graphologists or Handwriting Analysts.

Baseline - ⌊baseline⌋ is the ⌊real line⌋ or ⌊imaginary line⌋ that letters are written on.

x-height - is the height of $x or any letter without an ascender and descender $aceimnorsuvwxz

Letter Zones -

Head Zone — ascender
Body Zone — x-height
Leg Zone — descender

Upper zone ↑bdfhklt is called the head zone or ascender. It shows how a person thinks about ideas.

Middle zone →ghx is called body zone or x-height. It shows how a person communicates and interacts with others.

Lower zone ↳gjpqy is called leg zone or descender. It shows how a person does their physical actions.

A-Z Stories

of

Iggy   &   Peony

1. abc me

Iggy wrote her homework letters in less than a minute.

abc abc abc abc abc abc abc abc abc

Iggy felt this homework was much too easy for third grade, even if it was only the first day.

Iggy was already a good printer. She had expected homework practicing cursive like her big sister Peony had in third grade. But Iggy's teacher said all their class writing would be printed. Iggy was very disappointed.

Iggy thought of all the times Peony said cursive was smarter than printing. Iggy wanted to learn cursive to prove she was as smart as Peony. And more than that, she wanted to prove she was smart enough to read the cursive Peony wrote in her pink notebook.

Peony slid her finger over Iggy's writing and said, "Your deep press on paper shows you naturally press everything you learn deep into your brain. That's the clue for a strong memory."

Iggy wished her brain already knew as much as Peony and asked, "Doesn't everyone have a deep press?"

"No," said Peony tapping the first abc. "Most people press lighter." Then she asked, "Does your new teacher allow writing in green?"

"Why wouldn't she?" asked Iggy. "Green is for my name Iguana, like pink is for your name Peony."

Peony nodded and said, "That's true. Except this year my eighth grade teachers told us to only use black or blue in class. At least I can still use pink after school in the Handwriting Clues Club."

The mention of the Handwriting Clues Club made Iggy even more disappointed. She wished she could join and learn what Peony knew about handwriting. The problem was so many students wanted to be in it that Ms. Loops, the club teacher, required new members to already know cursive. She turned to Peony and said, "You're not really smarter just because you know cursive and I don't."

"It's cursive that's smarter," said Peony, pointing to Iggy's writing. "Look at the space between your *ab* To make that space you have to lift the pen and put it down again. That lift wastes time. Not wasting time by connecting letters is what's smarter and faster."

"I'm already smart and fast," said Iggy. "My teacher last year said I was the best speller and fastest writer in the class."

Peony shrugged and said, "If you think you're as smart as you can be, that's pink fine with me." Peony not only liked writing in pink, she liked highlighting what she said by saying the word pink.

Iggy thought of using her green highlighter over her abc's to highlight her strong press when Peony asked, "Did you take my notebook? It's not on the couch where I left it."

Iggy suddenly felt her lips squeeze together. She had taken that notebook and hid it under the couch cushion. She did it because she was mad at Peony for not letting her try to read the cursive writing in it. Iggy swallowed hard to keep inside what she had done, and said, "Me? Why would I take your notebook?"

Peony pointed to Iggy's $\mathcal{Q}$ and said, "Your secret loop $\mathcal{Q}\leftarrow$ shows you keep feelings and thoughts to yourself. That means I can't know everything you're thinking."

Iggy looked at the loop on her $\mathcal{Q}$ and didn't see anything wrong. In fact, she wanted to prove her $\mathcal{Q}$ was exactly right. She said, "Let's see you write it."

Peony wrote it twice, a a, saying, "Writing changes slightly every time you write.

Iggy immediately pointed to the second $a\leftarrow$ and shouted, "See, a secret loop. Mine is right!"

"Loops are not right or wrong," said Peony. "They simply show a person keeps some of their thoughts secret or private. But my secret loops are smaller than yours and I don't write them as often as you do. That shows you keep more to yourself than I do."

Peony glanced at the couch for a moment, then said, "You sure you didn't take my notebook?"

"No," snapped Iggy, then added as sweetly as she could, "I can't read cursive why would I take it?"

"Right here," said Peony tapping Iggy's writing, "your ℓ shows there is something on your mind you won't tell because you know it's wrong. Ms. Loops calls it being evasive or sneaky."

"Where?" Iggy demanded, suddenly scared she was caught.

Peony pointed and said, "The line at the beginning of your $\ell\leftarrow$ shows you're hiding what's really on your mind, a definite sneaky c."

"I am not a sneaky c!" shouted Iggy, "Writing your story in cursive is what's sneaky!"

Mom called into the room, "Iggy, Peony, why don't you girls write quietly in your notebooks. We'll have dinner soon."

"We will," Peony called back, then wrote, $c\,c$, in Iggy's notebook. "See this line," Peony said pointing to her second $c\leftarrow$.

Iggy bounced in her seat shouting, "Sneaky c!"

"My sneaky line starts with a curve, not an angle like yours so it's a gentle sneaky instead of an angry sneaky," said Peony, "And right now I'm gently sneaking this chat away from sneaky c to get you to try cursive. You will learn more clues from your cursive than your print because loops used in cursive give extra clues. Now try to connect letters like this."

Iggy felt better knowing Peony also had a sneaky c. And she felt much better for a chance to learn cursive.

Peony wrote *abc*.
Then Iggy tried and it came out *abc*.

"Mine's awful," said Iggy and reached to cross it out.

"Leave it," said Peony, "it's a good try."

Iggy didn't see anything good about it and said, "My hand feels stuck and doesn't know how to get to the next letter."

Peony nodded and said, "It is stuck until you learn your best way to connect them. With practice your hand will feel like it's sliding on whipped cream. Are you pink ready?"

"Green ready," said Iggy, raising her pen.

Peony put a cursive practice book on the table and said, "Trace this *abc* ten times, then practice in your notebook. Your own writing will be different than the traced letters because your hand will automatically write in your own natural style. All that matters is that someone else can read your letters as a, b and c."

Iggy traced the _abc_ ten times, then began writing in her notebook. She tried connecting letters with a bottom curve ↗ and tried making the b loop curve ∩ like in her traced letters. But as hard as she tried, her curves went straight _abc_.

She remembered Peony said her hand would write in her own natural style. She tried a straighter bottom connection and a smaller loop _abc_ . That felt more comfortable for her hand but still not right.

After many many more tries Iggy finally felt her hand slide into a smooth feeling _abc_.

She did it again and again and again. Then Iggy yelled, "Peony, come see, it feels like sliding on whipped cream!"

Peony came and watched Iggy write a smooth _abc_ .

"Pink penmanship prize for you," said Peony, "look at your smart, fast cursive."

"Am I smarter and faster than you?" asked Iggy.

"Faster will come with more practice because you do everything extra fast," said Peony. "Smarter depends on what you're being smart about. Let's see what shows in both of our abc's."

Peony pointed at Iggy's *b* and wrote *b* next to it.

"Look," said Peony, "Your b loop is taller and narrower than mine. Taller shows you spend more time thinking about ideas."

"I think more than you," said Iggy, sure this proved she was smarter than Peony.

"You do think a lot," said Peony, "Now look at the width. Narrow loop shows your thinking sticks to a few selected facts and doesn't consider anything else. Wide loop shows thinking with a lot of imagination, imagining many possibilities of what could be."

Iggy had to think about that for a moment, then asked, "Does that mean when I think about building the tallest tower for the school skyline contest I think of a a few towers I already selected, but your wide loop thinks of many more possible tall towers?"

"Pink right," said Peony. "See how easily you figured that out? Tall b stems also show you understand new ideas very easily and quickly. You are very smart."

Iggy felt extra proud of herself and asked, "Smarter than you?"

"Taller is not always smarter," said Peony. "It takes looking at the whole writing to see all the ways a person is smart. Sometimes a person with tall b's does things that are not smart at all."

"I'm always smart," said Iggy, "I will figure out how to build the tallest skyline tower the school has ever seen."

"You do win a lot at contests," said Peony, then pointed to both c's *c←* *c←* and asked, "is sneakier smarter?"

"That's not fair," said Iggy upset at being called sneaky again. Iggy put her finger over her *c* and said, "Your sneaky c is just as sneaky as mine."

Peony pointed to Iggy's finger and said, "Look more carefully for yourself."

Iggy hesitated, then moved her finger to look again at *c←* and *c←*.

Peony continued, "Yours is sneakier for three reasons. Your sneaky line is longer, straight, and starts with a sharp angle. Do you want me to explain?"

Iggy didn't like hearing so many reasons and wanted to tell Peony no. But at the same time, she had to learn what Peony knew. She tightened her lips and nodded.

Peony pointed to Iggy's *c* and said, "The straight line shows there is a plan in your mind that you want to keep hidden from others. The top of the line has an angle which shows the plan started with feeling angry. Being angry easily leads to doing something wrong or bad. My sneaky line *c* starts with a curve which shows mine starts with a feeling of concern. My sneaky is hiding something I know if I tell, it will make someone else feel bad. Both are sneaky because they don't tell the whole truth. But sneaky c that starts with anger usually hides things they do that they know are bad."

Iggy squeezed tight on her green pen and asked, "Does my angry angle sneaky c mean I'm very bad?"

"Pink no!" said Peony shaking her head. "It's a clue for you to see that your angle of anger gets your sneaky c started. But we need to look at clues in more than one letter to see the bigger picture of what gets your sneaky started."

"Can you see it in my *abc*?" asked Iggy.

"Pink yes," said Peony, "Do you want me to show you?"

Iggy didn't want Peony to find out she hid the notebook, but she really did want to know all that Peony saw in her abc. She slowly nodded her head yes.

"We'll examine your letters in order," began Peony, pointing to each letter as she spoke about them.

"*a* has a loop. Looking with this magnifying glass *a* you can see it better. It shows you keep secrets or private thoughts you don't want others to know. Do you?" Iggy shrugged but knew she did.

"*h* with a tall stem shows you think a lot and learn easily which is great. The narrow loop shows your thinking sticks to facts and doesn't use imagination. That's fine except it also means you don't imagine what other people are thinking, is that right?" Again Iggy shrugged, though she knew it never occurred to her to imagine what other people were thinking.

"And *c* with a line at the beginning shows hiding something in your mind that you don't want to say. The line starts with an angle which shows it started with feeling angry. Since it started with feeling angry, and anger makes people do wrong things, it's most likely something you know is wrong. Are you hiding something you know is wrong?"

Iggy shrugged again, though she knew it was yes and said, "Let me put the facts together. I keep secrets, I don't stop to imagine what other people are thinking, and there's something I'm hiding I know is wrong."

"Yes, exactly right," said Peony, "Is that you?"

Iggy knew it was her and none of it sounded smart. But what bothered her most was that she never stopped to imagine other people thought things that she didn't. Did Peony think something that she didn't? She had to find out and asked, "Peony, why won't you let me read your story?"

"That's pink important for you to know," said Peony nodding. "It's because I'm writing a story that I want to keep to myself until it's finished. For now it's my secret, really not a secret but just private for me until I'm ready to show it to others. I also have 2 other reasons."

Iggy was surprised there were even more reasons that she never imagined and asked, "What are those?"

Peony touched Iggy's notebook and said, "When I said you can't read my story, what I meant is you can't read it until you learn cursive. My reason #2 is to make you want to learn cursive."

"I do want to learn cursive," said Iggy, surprised that Peony was not trying to keep cursive to herself to act smarter. Then Iggy asked, "And what's reason #3?"

"Three is the most important to me," Peony began, then glanced at the couch before going on. "Once you can read cursive you can read my story by yourself, without hearing it through someone else's voice. Then you can tell me if the story is good or bad."

Iggy was even more surprised by this reason and asked, "What I think of your story tells if it's good or bad?"

"Pink sure," said Peony, "you're very smart in what you think of stories."

Iggy liked hearing Peony say she was very smart, but it made her feel terrible she took Peony's notebook. She asked, "Can a person with a bad sneaky c tell if a story is good?"

Peony smiled and said, "Your sneaky c is not bad. When people don't naturally imagine what others think and they think they're treated wrong, their mind sticks with that. But once they imagine there could be other reasons and ask, they usually find out the person wasn't treating them wrong at all. Then they don't need to be sneaky anymore."

Iggy was relieved that she didn't need to be sneaky anymore and rushed to get the notebook from under the couch cushion. She handed it to Peony, feeling her cheeks get hot as she said, "Sorry I took it but I wasn't smart enough to imagine your reasons. I won't hide your notebook ever again, I promise."

Peony hugged her notebook and said, "If you practice every day I'll teach you more clues that explain why you do what you do."

"I will," said Iggy, feeling so excited she jumped in a circle shouting, "My a b c tells a lot about me and soon I'll know more handwriting clues from Peony!"

"Dinnertime," called Mom.

The girls went to the table and Iggy said, "This is my favorite pizza, nutritionally smart whole grain crust, with extra nutritionally smart mushrooms and olives on top."

"Something has you in a good mood," said Mom with a big smile.

"Something I learned from Peony today. You want to know what?" asked Iggy to both her mom and sister.

"What?" they both asked at the same time.

Iggy pointed to her plate and announced, "The clues in my cursive writing are like the toppings on this pizza. They make something smart so much smarter."

Iggy took a big bite of pizza and began to bounce up and down in her seat while she chewed. Then she swallowed and said, "There's one more fact to add.

You want to hear it?"

Mom and Peony both nodded.

Iggy then announced, "My *abc* also taught me that considering more possibilities feels better than being a sneaky *c*."

Peony and her mom laughed while Iggy smiled wider. She couldn't wait to learn to write smarter and learn more smart handwriting clues. Third grade would be her cursive learning year after all.

2. defg me

defg defg defg defg defg

Iggy practiced defg in cursive over and over again for ten minutes. But her 13 year old sister Peony, and Peony's friend Raven, never said, 'Your cursive writing is great.' They were only interested in making butternut squash soup. Iggy finally pushed her notebook next to Peony at the stove and said proudly, "Look how great I am."

Raven came to look over Peony's shoulder and said, "I see some extra tall d's in there." They both laughed.

Iggy felt teased and shouted, "My extra tall d 's are for extra smart."

"Extra tall is not extra smart, especially in d's," said Raven while walking back to her mixing bowl.

Iggy knew that her tall b's showed she thinks a lot and learns new ideas easily, which is one way of being smart. She was upset to be wrong and asked, "If tall is smart then why doesn't extra tall mean extra smart?"

"If I tell you, will you let us finish this recipe?" asked Peony.

"Sure," said Iggy, "You think I like being near your smelly soup?"

Peony patted Iggy's shoulder, then wrote $b\ b$.

"That's tall and extra tall b," Peony said pointing to the letters. "Tall b shows learns ideas easily. Extra tall b also shows learns ideas easily with the extra tall part meaning the ideas they think about go farther away from what is real into made up theories, like what life on other planets looks like. All extra tall stems show the person adds theoretical guesses to their ideas, except for d."

Iggy watched Peony write tall and extra tall *ℓ* *ℓ*, then asked, "Why is d different?"

Peony pointed to tall *ℓ* and said, "Stem in d shows how you feel about yourself. Tall *ℓ* stem means you feel proud of what you do and want others proud of you, too."

Iggy nodded her head and said, "That's me, proud *d*. I am proud of what I do and I like hearing others say they're proud of me. Isn't that part of smart?"

"Being proud of yourself is great," began Peony, "but shows how you feel about yourself, not how easily you learn new ideas. A d stem that goes at least 3 times taller than the circle *ℓ* is extra tall made up thinking about how you feel about yourself. See the different heights in your *d* and *d* ?"

Iggy looked and saw her second stem was at least 3 times taller than the circle.

"The extra tall one," Peony said, "is called great-me-d. Stem in d shows how you feel about yourself. Extra tall d-stem shows you feel you are extra great and that you deserve extra tall attention for how great you are. It also shows you feel you don't get the extra tall attention you feel you deserve."

"That's a fact," said Iggy, "I am great-me-d and I don't get the extra tall attention I deserve."

Peony and Raven laughed again and Iggy shouted, "Don't think you're so great, you're only interested in stinky soups!"

"Calm down before your brain boils over," said Raven. "Take a look at Peony's d stem next to yours."

l d

Iggy looked and Raven continued, "See Peony's extra wide loop? Extra wide loop in d shows Peony's imagination makes up criticisms about herself all the time. Your extra tall d makes up that you should be told you're great all the time. Neither one of those d's is great to have. Besides, nobody's great all the time."

"I am!" shouted Iggy. She felt so teased and so mad, she stormed out of the room.

But then Iggy heard Peony say, "She is pink great at a lot of things. I feel bad that I'm too busy with homework and my Pink Ink Blog to tell her often enough."

"Iggy needs a lot of attention sure as soup needs a lot of salt," said Raven, "and you give her plenty. Don't criticize yourself so much. You're a fine big sister and have the most open minded taste buds of any friend I ever had. Now write this down. One teaspoon vanilla, one teaspoon cinnamon, one-half teaspoon curry, one-half teaspoon ginger, and one cup coconut milk."

It got quiet and Iggy knew Peony was writing the recipe that Raven made up while Raven mixed the ingredients in the bowl. That's what they did every Sunday afternoon. They called it taste bud science.

Iggy called it taste bud torture. No way would they get her to taste any of their soups. But she did want to hear what else Peony had to say about her. She sat outside the kitchen door and waited.

Iggy heard Peony tap her pen on the counter and say, "It's pink great Iggy practices cursive every day. And she has some open e's to show she'll listen to what she wants to learn."

Iggy quickly looked at the e's in her notebook.

defy defy defy defy defy

Some were like an i without the dot...

defy

others had a loop with some space in it.

defy defy

Were the e loops with some space her open e's?

"And her other handwriting clues," Peony said, "she has nice think & do f's, I'm proud she can think and do things for herself."

"The open e's and f's are excellent ingredients in her," said Raven, "even her pushy g adds to what she can do."

Iggy couldn't wait a moment longer to know what they meant. She rushed inside demanding, "Tell me about my e's, f's and g's," then she added sweetly, "please?"

Raven held up her spoon and said, "If you wait and watch, I'll mix and tell."

"Okay, I'm waiting," said Iggy and watched Raven carefully lift her bowl of brown mixture over the pot of orange mush.

"Look at that," said Raven slowly stirring the brown into an e shape that had a loop with big space in it. "This is open e. It shows listening with open ears."

"Open e looks like an ear," said Iggy, touching her own ear and waiting to hear what else Raven had to say.

Raven used her spoon to make a brown f with long top and bottom loops *f*. "That's think & do *f*," she said. "The top is for how much you think *f* and the bottom is for how much action you do *f*. People who write two long loops think up lots of ideas and then do them, like me."

Iggy made a sour face at Raven and said, "You put pickles on peanut butter, who wants to think and do that?"

"That's your pinched e talking," said Raven, spooning the shape *e*. "Pinched e shows ears that are closed to new ideas."

defy

Iggy thought of her e like an i without a dot, and knew she sometimes did that.

Raven mixed the rest of the brown until it blended with the orange squash. Iggy thought it smelled weird.

Raven ladled some of her soup into 3 small bowls and said to Iggy, "Ready for your taste?"

Iggy wrinkled her nose and said a quick, "No way!"

Raven wrinkled her nose back and said, "Should I say no way to telling about your g?"

Iggy didn't like the choice she had to make, but she did know what was most important to her. She felt her throat get tight and said, "If I have to try it I want the smallest spoon in the house."

Peony laughed and handed her the green baby spoon from the drawer, saying, "This tiny spoon matches the size of your g loop."

Peony pointed to Iggy's → 𝒴 .

Iggy realized there could be much more than pushy to know about g and immediately shoved the tiny spoon in her mouth. It tasted awful and she wished she could spit it out. But the thought of insulting Raven and not hearing all about her g was worse. Iggy swallowed as fast as she could.

"Delicious, right?" asked Raven.

Iggy forced her face into a half smile and said, "I would call it swamp soup."

Raven frowned at first, but then smiled as she said, "Like it or not you did taste it. Now it's your g time."

Raven pointed to Iggy's → γ and said, "The leg loop shows if your will-try list is wide or narrow. Yours is narrow meaning you don't want to try new tastes."

"I don't like new tastes or soups," said Iggy. "I like tomato soup and that's it. Don't even try to get me to taste your other soups."

Raven laughed and said, "And that's the reason you aren't as extra smart as you think you are. Extra smart means learning everything you can to make you smarter, not just facts but also tastes."

Iggy didn't like Raven repeating that she wasn't extra smart. She would prove how smart she was by asking smart questions. She examined her narrow loop and asked, "Is that a pinched g, like my pinched e's?"

"Not the same," began Raven, "Pinched means two lines written on top of each other that look like one line. Show her Peony."

Peony wrote next to Iggy's g.

γ q

Raven continued, "Yours has a very narrow loop which shows if there's a very good reason you will try a little."

24

"I did try a little," said Iggy proudly. "My pinched e didn't want to but my narrow g loop had a good reason."

"That's right," said Raven nodding. "Pinched e doesn't want to hear about it but your narrow g gave you a narrow opening to change that no to a yes."

"I get it," said Iggy. "Also, some of my e's are open." She pointed proudly to both of her open e's...

defy defy

Iggy went on, "That means I sometimes want to try something by hearing about it, like hearing more about what g means."

Raven nodded and Iggy finally had a chance to ask, "Is narrow g the same as pushy g?"

Raven laughed and said, "Your open e's do listen! But the answer is no, narrow and pushy are not the same. Pushy g is the line that pushes forward, see it?"

Raven pointed g ← and Iggy nodded.

Raven went on, "Your pushy g means you push yourself hard to get things done. But beware because pushy also means if someone is in your way you could act pushy to them. And there's more."

Iggy started to cover her ears, afraid of hearing something else bad about herself. Raven shook her head and said, "Don't cover your ears now, the rest is all good."

Iggy realized what she had done and put her hands behind her ears to hold them out as she said, "Wide open and ready."

Raven pointed to the pushy leg and said, "Your pushy leg is also nicely long. Legs that are long below the baseline mean you stick with your interests and work at them for a long time without wanting to stop. Your sister is like that, too, but different." Raven turned to Peony and said, "Show her your g."

Peony wrote her g next to Iggy's g.

Iggy looked at Peony's wide leg loop. She never realized she and Peony were so different in what they were willing to try and shouted, "No wonder Peony will taste all of your crazy recipes, her will-try list is wide!"

Peony laughed and said to Raven, "I told you Iggy is pink smart."

"Two sisters, one's first will-try reaction is no, and the other is a wide open yes. But the great thing about you both is you both have long leg g's. That shows you both stick with actively doing your interests for a long time and you both get what's important to you done."

Iggy always liked hearing something about her was great and said, "I work a long time on lots of things. Just ask Peony how much I practice writing. I also spend hours learning about all kinds of animals and then make up my own games."

"You, my dear Iggy, certainly do have many great ingredients," said Raven, "even when you think people don't notice how great you are. That's how I feel about my soups. I think they're great and I can't understand why others don't constantly say they're great, too. You sure you don't want to try it again?"

Iggy's nose automatically wrinkled and Peony said, "Raven, her g loops are narrow, that's how she is. But I'm ready for my taste."

Peony dipped a large spoon in her bowl and then slipped it into her mouth. Peony's eyes opened wider as she said, "Mmm, savory blend of flavors and texture. The headline in my next Pink Ink Blog will be, *Raven's Squash Soup is a Big Splash of Taste and Texture.*"

Iggy couldn't think of any part of the soup that was good and wanted to change the subject back to her. She asked, "Do my other letters also show I don't like trying new foods?"

Peony shook her head and said, "Different clues in each letter explain different parts of you that all work together. Let's look at today's letters," and pointed to

defy

Peony then raised a new finger for each letter as she said,

1. "Extra tall great-me *d* shows you always want to hear you're great. But you also have tall *d* that shows you know you achieve a lot to feel proud of, even if others don't say you're great.
2. Pinched *e* shows there are times you just don't want to listen, but sometimes you write open *e* which shows you do listen if you're interested.
3. Think and do *f* with long loops show you are good at thinking up new ideas and then doing them.
4. Narrow loop *y* shows if it's not already on your will-try list, then you won't try it without an

important reason to you. But the long g leg shows you work long amounts of time on what does interest you.

5. Putting it all together, you do achieve a lot to be proud of, you do listen to what you want to hear, you do work for long times at what interests you, but you don't see any reason to take time to consider new things to try, unless maybe if it's to hear others say you're great. Is that why you tried the taste?"

Iggy nodded at all she just heard and shouted,

"*defg* that's me!"

Then she asked, "Does considering a new food make a narrow g leg person extra great?"

"Quick as instant noodles," said Raven, "at least to me it does. All you have to do is think up a new food to try and it's on my will-do list."

Iggy was amazed how all it took was deciding to think about it and an exciting will-try idea came to her fast. She announced to Raven, "If you make tomato soup I'll try it, because I know I like canned tomato soup. I'll even taste it with a big spoon."

"What an interesting idea," said Raven, "My own tomato soup and since it's for Iggy I'll add green spinach alphabet pasta. That's next week's taste bud science."

"Sounds tasty to me," said Peony. "Sound good to you, Iggy?"

Iggy didn't know what green spinach pasta tasted like but instead of saying a pinched or narrow loop no, she said, "You know what?"

"What?" Peony and Raven asked at the same time.

Iggy pointed to her notebook and said, "I will try it because my defg clues say great me is really greater if I consider a new taste. I also will try it because learning new tastes is extra smart!"

Peony and Raven laughed for a long time, not a teasing laugh, but an approving laugh. And Iggy was proud of herself for getting this extra attention which did make her feel extra great.

3. hijk me

Iggy struggled to sit still and quiet. That whole day was NOT FAIR! It started with the awful things that happened at school. Now she couldn't say a word because Peony needed total concentration before her gymnastics team tryout.

Iggy didn't want to ruin Peony's concentration, but she, Iggy, also had things on her mind. In fact, what happened to her was all she could think about. She had built the highest tower ever in her class, as practice for the skyline building contest, and couldn't wait for the teacher to see it. But before her teacher had a chance to look, that awful boy Keko kicked it. All 289 blocks that Iggy so carefully put together, crashed down to the floor. Keko laughed at the fallen tower and Iggy gave him a shove. And because of that one little push, she had to sit in the quiet corner for fifteen whole minutes while Keko didn't get any punishment at all. It was so unfair!

Peony watched Marcia do her floor routine and said, "I wish my leg kicked that high."

Iggy heard the words kicked and high and couldn't stop herself any longer. She whispered a little too loudly, "Keko kicked down my highest tower!"

"You promised to keep quiet," said Peony, still watching Marcia. "Write it down and show me later. For now there's no talking, Iggy, I mean it." Then Peony pinched her lips tight.

Iggy knew about Peony's pinched lips. They meant if Iggy didn't stay quiet, Peony would not talk to her for a long time, maybe a whole week. Iggy couldn't take that chance. She had too much she had to tell Peony, that is once she was allowed to speak. She opened her notebook and stared at it. Usually she liked writing and practiced cursive writing every day. She also liked when Peony explained the reasons she did things by looking at the way she wrote her letters. This time she just felt angry. She jabbed her pen on the paper and wrote,

I made the highest tower in the class and

Peony's name was called and Iggy stopped writing to watch. Peony began with a perfect split on the bar, stood into a perfectly balanced half turn, then held a perfectly steady arabesque. Peony looked amazing and Iggy was sure Peony would be chosen for the team. Except then on dismount, Peony lost her balance and ended up on the floor. Peony looked more surprised than hurt and quickly stood with her arms in the air. She kept her mouth in a smile all the way back to her seat. But once she sat down, she looked ready to cry.

Iggy felt sorry for her sister and said, "The ending wasn't so bad and you're much better than Marcia. She looks stiff while you look graceful."

But Peony just shook her head and mumbled, "Not now, stay quiet."

Iggy wanted to talk so badly, in fact she wanted to scream so badly, but instead she bit her lip. Her hand returned to writing when she suddenly stopped. She needed to ask how to spell the word 'unfair' only she wasn't allowed to speak. She guessed at the spelling though she hated to guess. She liked to know things for sure.

Peony suddenly spoke in a sorrowful voice, "It's not fair. I practiced and practiced and practiced and still made that mistake."

"A lot of things are not fair!" Iggy couldn't stop herself from yelling out loud.

Peony's mouth went tight, but Iggy couldn't hold back any longer and said in a lower voice, "I can't be quiet another second no matter what you do."

Peony let out a long breath and said, "Okay, what's your problem, I'm listening."

"Keko," Iggy started, but then tears rushed down her face and she couldn't speak. She held out her notebook and said, "It's all here."

I made the highest tower
in the class and jerk
Keko knocked it down!

Peony looked at it while shaking her head, then suddenly began to laugh.

"It's not funny!" shrieked Iggy.

"I'm not laughing at what you wrote," said Peony, "I'm laughing at how you wrote it. Here, take a look."

Iggy couldn't understand how her handwriting clues were funny since she felt so bad.

Peony pointed at the first h in the word highest. "See this 𝓵 stem is taller and wider than all your other 𝓵 stems? It's extra tall and wide for extra feelings about wanting extra notice for some extra achievement. Do you remember what I told you yesterday?"

"Yes," said Iggy, feeling better at the chance to show off her good memory. "You said that when letters are much taller or wider than you usually write them, the word those letters are in is a clue. And the word here is highest." Iggy underlined her four h's...

the highest the

"Pink perfect memory," said Peony. "The different way you wrote the beginning h in *highest* clearly shows you had a lot of extra feelings and wanted extra notice for your achievement connected to that word. The word *highest* was extra important to you."

"It was extra-extra important to me!" said Iggy.

Peony tapped on that h and said, "The extra big size clue shows it perfectly. You were extra proud that it was the highest and couldn't wait to hear your teacher say how great it was."

"Yes," said Iggy, remembering Peony explain her extra tall d's. Those showed she definitely wanted to hear how great she was.

"And do you see the lines instead of dots over your *i*'s and *j*?" asked Peony.

"They look like bee stingers," said Iggy thinking of when she was stung by a bee and how much it hurt.

"That's right," said Peony. "When people feel bad like they were stung by a bee they make a bee stinger on the page instead of a dot. Is that how you felt?"

"It was," said Iggy, feeling stung just thinking about it.

"Now look at this," Peony said pointing to the word *jerk*. "The leg of this *j* pushes forward instead of going back to make a loop like you do in your → *y*. Going back to make a loop, even a narrow loop like yours, shows taking time to think about it. But this *j* shows you didn't take any time to think at all. With feeling bad like you were stung by a bee you pushed right into your next action without thinking. You could easily have been mad enough to really push someone. Did you?"

Iggy blurted out, "I pushed Keko and he fell down!"

"I thought so," said Peony, her face wincing like she was remembering her own fall. Peony began speaking again, "Legs show the kind of actions we automatically take, even if they're not what we want them to be. That's why taking the time to think is important. The line straight forward in your *j-k* shows your physical action can automatically get physically aggressive. When you get mad you have to be careful not to do anything wrong."

Iggy didn't feel she had done anything wrong and shouted, "But Keko was the one who was wrong and I was the one who got punished. It's not fair!"

Peony nodded her head and said, "Yes, that's right here, too."

"What is?" asked Iggy.

"Look at your *k*'s," said Peony. "Your k arm pushes high up above your x-height *k←x*. A k-arm pushed up above the x-height is called defiant-k and looks like raising your fist in the air. Defiant-k shows you are extra quick to say, *It's not fair!*"

Iggy looked closely at her *k*'s in

jerk   Keko   knocked

It was true her k arms went above her x-height like a fist in the air. Seeing it actually made her feel even stronger how unfair she had been treated and she shouted, "But it wasn't fair!"

"It was unfair that Keko kicked down your tower," said Peony. "But take a pink think minute. If you had not pushed him down, your teacher would have punished him and not you. Wouldn't that have been better?"

Iggy had to take a few moments to think about that. In her mind it still wasn't fair, but Peony did have a point. Iggy finally said, "It would have been more fair if Keko got punished. But it was extra unfair that my teacher didn't see my tower."

"Pink right it was," said Peony, "but before you say anything to your teacher, think of your handwriting clues to know why you did what you did."

Iggy couldn't remember all that Peony had said and asked, "Can you explain them to me again?"

"Sure I can," said Peony and pointed to letters as she spoke,

"Extra tall and wide k loop, bigger than your usual k, shows extra feelings and thoughts about making the highest tower in your class, which means you were extra proud to show your teacher, and also extra disappointed when Keko kicked it down.

Bee stinger dots ⊂ ⌐ show how bad you felt.

Aggressive ⌐ leg shows you didn't stop to think like you sometimes do before taking action."

𝑘 arm in the air shows you are extra-quick to say 'it's not fair'. And one more k clue is no loop in your stem to the head 𝑘 like this 𝑘. Do you see that?"

Iggy nodded and Peony said, "No stem loop in cursive k shows not taking the time to consider other thinking possibilities, like what's on your teacher's mind." Peony looked up at Iggy and said, "Those are your clues. How would you put them together?"

Iggy thought about the extra big ℎ loop, bee stinger dots ⊂ ⌐, aggressive leg ⌐, and fist in the air no stem loop 𝑘, then said, "I was extra excited to build the tower, then extra upset at Keko and didn't stop to think before pushing him. And I didn't think at all what was on my teacher's mind. Maybe she didn't see Keko knock down the tower but she did see me push him. I'll ask her tomorrow and ask if 1 can have another chance to build the tower. And I'll ask if she can keep Keko on the other side of the room when I build it."

Peony laughed and said, "You not only understand why you did what you did, you found a great solution."

Mom returned from shopping to pick them up and asked, "Everything okay, girls?"

Iggy jumped up and said, "Peony had a bad ending on the balance beam but she made a great ending to my day."

Peony smiled and said, "That's fair enough for me."

Iggy walked out of the gym feeling happy and decided to write a note to Peony, signing her name Iggy with j's instead of g's, making sure the legs had loops and the dots didn't push into bee stingers. And she'd loop the k stem. Peony would surely know what all that meant.

Thank you!
Ijjy ☮

"You know what's not fair?" asked Iggy as they drove in the car.

"What?" asked Mom and Peony at the same time.

Iggy said, "It's not fair that everyone doesn't have a sister like Peony. She passed the tryout for the smartest big sister today with her smart handwriting clues."

Peony and Mom laughed and Iggy knew that with all the things that went wrong that day, she had just done something right.

At that moment Mom's phone rang and a voice came into the car, "Mrs. Pensky, this is Peony's coach. I'm happy to say Peony made the team and is to report to practice on Saturday."

Iggy was so excited that when the call ended Iggy yelled, "You did it, can I come and watch? I'll sit quietly, and won't push my j's at anyone or raise my k fist no matter what happens. Can I, please?"

Peony turned around from the front seat and said, "Iggy, if you stayed quiet with all you went through today, then I know you'll be fine to watch me practice."

Iggy remembered how unfair it had felt to sit absolutely quiet. But now she realized it wasn't unfair because if staying quiet was important to Peony then it was just as important to her. She was proud that she had stopped to think and acted right. "You know what?" asked Iggy again.

"What?" asked Mom and Peony one more time.

Iggy bounced up and down on her seat and said, "Today I passed an important team tryout, too. I made it to the younger sister can act fair and fine team!"

Mom and Peony laughed and Iggy felt all really was fair most of the time, and when it wasn't she would try her hardest to make it fair in the end.

4. lmno me

"That's not true!" Iggy yelled at the TV. This was
almost as bad as that morning when her teacher
asked which insect they thought was most important.
Keko said spiders because they catch mosquitoes.
Iggy had wanted everyone to know the correct fact
and shouted, 'The most important insects are bees
because they pollinate 85% of our food. Without bees
we would starve to death.' But her teacher ignored
that important fact and told her to listen quietly to
what others had to say. That was so unfair. Facts are
either right or wrong, and correct facts are what's
most important.

Iggy was proud that she knew a lot of facts. The
importance of facts even showed in her handwriting.

43

Her sister Peony had explained that when they compared their l's *l* *l*. Iggy's narrow loop *l* shows her thinking sticks to the facts. Peony's wide loop *l* shows she thinks with lots of imagination.

Peony walked into the room and asked, "Why are you yelling at the TV?"

Iggy pointed to the screen and said, "That commercial for Bumble Bee Honey doesn't know the facts. Bumblebees only make enough honey for themselves. It's honeybees that make extra for us humans to eat. They should call it Honeybee Honey, not Bumblebee. Bees are not all the same."

Peony usually agreed with Iggy's opinions of commercials. This time Peony mumbled in a low voice, "Just like m's are not all the same."

"Of course m's are not all the same," said Iggy, "everyone writes letters differently."

Peony held up her handwritten essay and said, "According to Ms. Loops there are different kinds of m's which show different kinds of thinking. I only write one kind of m which is the wrong kind for an essay."

Those facts didn't make sense to Iggy and she said, "You got a B, isn't that good thinking?"

Peony shook her head and said, "B minus, not that good. Listen to what my teacher wrote. 'Strong summary of the history of hunger in Africa but doesn't state a specific problem and solution.' And when I showed it to Ms. Loops, she said, 'Look at your m's'."

"That's not fair," said Iggy. "You had a strong summary, what else does your teacher want?"

"She wants the facts, then a solution based on those facts. I have to figure it out and do a rewrite," said Peony starting up the steps to her room.

Iggy held up the stack of index cards she wrote yesterday, one for each bee fact she knew, and said, "Play Buzzy Bees with me."

"Not now," called Peony from above.

Iggy rushed up the steps after her. But before Iggy reached the top, Peony closed her door. Iggy quickly solved the problem of the closed door by shouting into it, "What are the different bees in a hive? And you have to say Buzzy Bee before the answer."

Iggy waited a moment for a reply but none came. Iggy shouted the answer, "Buzzy Bee, the different bees in the hive are the queen, the drones, and the workers."

There was absolutely no sound from Peony. Iggy felt challenged by the silence and was determined to be heard. This time she shouted louder through the door, "What do the different bees do?"

Again there was no answer from Peony, and again Iggy shouted the answer, "Buzzy Bee, the queen lays eggs, the drones fertilize the eggs, and the workers collect pollen to make the honey that feeds them all."

Iggy shouted another question even louder, "Tell me the most important members of the hive, the queen, the drones, or the workers?"

Iggy started to shout the answer, when she noticed most of her m's had points on both top and bottom.

Tell me the most important members of the hive?

Then she noticed some were rounded instead of pointy. It was true that there were many kinds of m's. Suddenly she had to know what they all meant. Iggy pounded on the door yelling, "Buzzy Bee, I need to know about my m's, can you please tell me now?"

The door opened and Peony stood there gripping the handle. "Okay Buzzy Bee," Peony began, "what's so important it can't wait?"

"What do points on my m's mean?" asked Iggy handing Peony the card.

Tell me the most important members of the hive?

Peony read for a minute, her mouth tightening the way it did when she was upset. Then she shook her head and said, "For pink's sake, you sure do need to know."

"What's wrong?" asked Iggy, thinking Peony's shaking head meant she saw something bad.

"Your writing," said Peony, "it's just like Ms. Loops showed us in Handwriting Clues Club. It's your m's in the words *most important members*"

Iggy looked at the variety of points and humps.

"This point down," said Peony putting her finger at the beginning of *most* "shows you see problems and solutions very quickly. You take facts like bumblebees don't make extra honey and honeybees do make extra honey. You then instantly see the problem with the name Bumblebee Honey and quickly solve it by changing the name to Honeybee Honey."

"Is that wrong?" asked Iggy.

"Wrong no, it's actually pink smart," began Peony moving her finger slightly, "Then you have lots of points up ⌢ that show natural curiosity. That's why I said you sure do need to know because you have so many."

Iggy was always curious to know more about things that interested her. Two weeks ago it was iguanas of which out of the 13 species her favorite was green. Last week it was peonies which out of 3000 varieties her favorite was sea shell pink. This week she's most interested in bees. Except right now at this exact moment, her biggest interest is m's.

Iggy pointed to the first m in the word members and asked, "Does that round top m mean I don't want to know more?"

Peony shook her head and said, "The round shape is called a hump, like on a camel. It means taking your time to think more about what you already know."

"I do already know a lot about camels," said Iggy, always excited to show off her memorized facts. "If they fall in quicksand they don't move until they figure the best way to get out. Taking their time to think is smart, because if they move before they figure it all out, they go deeper in the quicksand and can't ever get out."

"That's a perfect explanation," said Peony, "sometimes slow thinking is the smarter choice. Slow thinking shown by m humps is also more creative because it means the person takes the time to consider lots of possibilities. But since most of your m's are pointy, your usual thinking is quick and too impatient for that. Your usual is to figure out a solution fast, then move on to something else. And now that you have your solution to your m's, you can quickly leave and move on to something else."

Peony leaned her head on her open door and Iggy realized she looked ready to cry. Iggy's points-up curiosity still wanted to learn more about m's. But more than that, she felt bad for Peony and wanted to make her feel better. She asked, "Why are you so sad?"

Peony looked at the floor and said, "You have so many down points that show you easily focus on facts to get to sharp, precise, and smart solutions of problems. I don't have those down points and find it very hard to do that. Even my little sister thinks better than me."

Iggy felt flattered and almost shouted, 'I'm smarter than you!' But she knew if she did that Peony would feel worse and she wanted to make Peony feel better.

Instead, Iggy said, "Peony, you're way smarter than me about lots of things. Look how many handwriting clues you know that I don't."

"I knew you would say that," said Peony. "That's in your m's, too."

"What is?" asked Iggy.

Peony pointed at the Buzzy Bee card in Iggy's hand. "See the first m in the word members → *members*. The second hump is lower than the first hump. That shows you notice when someone else feels lower than you and you want to raise their feelings."

"I do want to raise your feelings," said Iggy, "And remember what you said that pointy m's are fast thinking, but that fast is not always better. Like the smart camel who needs time to think their way out of quicksand, your hump thinking is smart, too."

Peony glanced at her paper with the B- on top and said, "Ms. Loops says my hump m's are great for the stories I write because slow thinking gives me time to use my big imagination. But she said some down point thinking is helpful for doing school work. She said I'll start to get some down points in my m's when I push myself hard to focus on the exact points of problems and their solutions.

Iggy looked from Peony's m's to her own and asked, "How do you know how many points and humps you want?"

Peony laughed and said, "It's not what you want, it's what you have. Your many down points show your mind naturally goes straight to the points of problems and solutions. My all hump thinking shows my mind naturally goes straight to my imagination. I have to work hard at doing what's easy for you. Ms. Loops says the more I practice focusing on facts to find the precise points to use to solve problems, the better at it I will be."

"The fact is," said Iggy, jumping up and down, "this bee question is perfect practice for you." She looked at her card and started, "Which honeybees are the most important to the hive, the Queen, the drones, or the workers? And remember you have to say Buzzy Bee before you answer."

Peony started to open her mouth, then shut it and turned away to her window. It was hard for Iggy to wait patiently but she knew Peony was thinking slowly to consider many possibilities and she had to give her that time.

Finally Peony said, "If the queen lays the eggs and the drones fertilize the queen, and the workers make the honey they all need to eat, then they are all important, you can't pick just one."

"That's right," shouted Iggy with excitement. "Just like you said about the different kinds of m's, all the different bees are important."

"That's it," said Peony, "the solution for my essay on hunger in Africa. There are three major problems. Those are irrigation for growing crops, machines for harvesting, and trucks to deliver the food. Those three problems require all three for the solution, where no one solution is more important than the others. They all have to work together for the solution to work."

Iggy started jumping up and down too excited to stand still. "See how smart your m humps are?"

Peony quickly wrote a few sentences on her essay page and said, "Look at that," she pointed to the old way she wrote n in *hunger* and then the one just now *hunger*. "The new n has a down point for solving problems. Did I tell you n's are like m's? Both m and n have humps or points to show how you think."

"Two thinking letters means we can have two thinking questions," said Iggy, "How do bees talk to each other?"

"Another question?" asked Peony, "Can't your mouth ever stop buzzing?"

"No," said Iggy surprised at the question. She liked hearing herself talk, especially when it was about interesting facts.

Peony took the card from Iggy's hand and said, "I should have noticed that clue right away, open o means open mouth."

most important

Iggy looked closely and saw her *o* was open on top. It looked right to her, like an open top on a bee hive with space for buzzing bees to fly in and out. She began buzzing and spinning around at the same time, then said, "I like to buzz, don't you?"

"Pink no," said Peony. "We're different in most ways. Now go buzz into another room and let me have some quiet."

Iggy was too curious about what Peony said to leave the room and asked, "How different are we?"

Peony took a deep breath, then began, "Just from yesterday and today we found lots of differences. Peony pointed to letters as she spoke,

"Your narrow loop *l* and my wide loop *l* show your mind sticks to the facts while my imagination is always part of my thinking.

My m's & n's are humps for slow thinking while you have w's and w's with many points up for big curiosity and points down for quick to get to the points of problems and solutions. Some of my m humps go lower like yours m m for noticing when others feel low and wanting to raise their feelings. But some of my m humps get higher M to show I sometimes feel others are better than me. Your m's don't do that which shows you don't ever feel that way."

"No one is better than me," said Iggy, "I'm the smartest one in my class."

Peony laughed and said, "I pink knew you would say what's on your mind, which brings us to o's. Your c's are open on top and mine are closed σ. You always want to talk and sometimes I don't want to talk at all."

Iggy did like to talk especially when there was more she wanted to know and asked, "Like when you go to your room and close the door?"

"You figured that out fast as always," said Peony. "Now can I be left alone?"

"The fact is," began Iggy, "I want to understand all these clues and I need your help. I know we think differently and at different speeds. And I always have to know more and like to open my mouth to ask while you don't always want to talk. But why do you sometimes think others are better than you?"

Peony stayed quiet for a few moments then said, "It's because I am slower that I think others are better. I can't be like the kids who raise their hand right away in class and know every answer. I'm sure you can do that."

Iggy nodded and said, "I can, and until just now I used to think others were not smart when they don't raise their hand or they give an answer I think is wrong. But now I realize they could be considering more possibilities that I didn't think of. Like maybe Keko thinks spiders are the most important insect because he gets a lot of itchy mosquito bites and spiders eat a lot of mosquitoes. Or the honey commercial, maybe there was already another company with the name Honeybee and they had to use the name Bumble Bee. It really is a fact that slow thinking for more possibilities is smart thinking, too."

Peony smiled and said, "You're right, I don't have to feel others are better than me just because they're fast and I'm slow. I can be pink proud of taking my time to consider everything in my big imagination. But it would help my essay to have a few down points."

Iggy started jumping up and down and said, "And you can practice with one more fact. Here's your question. How do bees communicate?"

"Okay Buzzy Bee," said Peony, "I suppose they communicate by buzzing."

"Right," said Iggy, "but bees also communicate by dancing. Just like there's more than one way to think, there's more than one way to communicate. And right now I'm shutting my mouth to dance into a hug to make you feel better." Iggy did a quick turn and held her arms open wide.

Peony picked up her little sister and twirled her around till they were so dizzy they lay down on the floor.

"After a few moments Iggy asked, "You know what?"

"No," said Peony, "but I'm sure you'll tell me."

Iggy said, "Teaching me the handwriting clues for my *Emma* taught me a lot about me and you. And the best thing I learned is that together our different ways of thinking can solve any problems that come our way!"

5. pqrs me

Brush forward, brush back, stomp. Brush forward, brush back, stomp. That Iggy could do, but then the tap class had to brush forward and go right into a high hop. Everyone in the class was able to do it but Iggy. How could her family be proud of her when she was the worst one on stage? She tried again and again and again, but lost her balance on every hop.

Daphne in front of her could do it right. Iggy was sure it was because Daphne was right behind the teacher. Iggy thought if she was right behind Ms. Tapiq then she could do it, too. She stomped her way next to Daphne, and because there wasn't enough space, she bumped into Daphne's arm.

"Go back, you're in my spot," said Daphne, her arm pressing back on Iggy.

Iggy wanted to push Daphne out of the way, but her big sister Peony told her pushing causes trouble. Peony said when angry, she should put her hands together and squeeze. Iggy squeezed her hands together and said, "This whole room is everyone's spot."

"No it's not," said Daphne. "This spot is mine."

Ms. Tapiq turned around and said, "Dancers don't argue, they smile and practice. Shall we continue, girls?"

Iggy didn't want Ms. Tapiq to think she was causing trouble and tried to keep her voice sweet as she said, "I can't see your feet from back there."

"Very well," said Ms. Tapiq, "if you need front row, go down to the end."

Iggy felt misunderstood and wanted to shout, but her mom had told her that shouting makes people mad. Mom said instead of shouting she should take a deep breath to calm down. Iggy took a deep breath and said as calmly as she could, "I can't see from down there. Why can't I stay here?"

"Because I'm here," said Daphne waving her arm in front of Iggy.

Seeing that arm almost hitting her face was too much for Iggy to remember to squeeze her hands or take a deep breath. This time Iggy pushed Daphne's arm and shouted, "I'm here too, and this is my spot as much as yours."

"Girls stop that!" said Ms. Tapiq, rushing between them and added in a firm voice, "Tap dancers always have a happy face for their audience. Say you're sorry, put on your smiles, and let's rehearse."

"I'm not sorry," said Daphne. "I didn't do anything wrong."

"I'm not sorry, either," said Iggy, feeling it was all so unfair. She tried not to sound as mad as she felt when she said, "I can't learn the steps from back there. Daphne can do it because she's right behind you."

"Girls, girls," said Ms. Tapiq without her usual smile, "dancers believe entertaining the audience always comes first. If you won't put on a happy face, you can't be on stage. Sit on the side and watch while the rest of us practice for next week's show. There's no more time to waste. The show must go on."

"But it's not fair," Iggy said, trying hard not to scream.

Ms. Tapiq raised a finger to stop Iggy from saying another word, then in a low but commanding voice said,

"When you're ready to smile for the audience, you can join us at the end of the first row."

Iggy absolutely could not smile at that moment, and absolutely could not give in to going to the end of the first row. Iggy went to the side of the room, sat on the floor, and because Peony had told her to write when she's mad, began to write in her notebook. She wrote,

page 22

Ms. Tapia is unfair

Daphne is unfair

Sitting quiet is unfair

I want to dance now!

Iggy watched the class walk to the left, then do heel toe, heel toe, heel toe. Next they walked to the right followed by toe heel, toe heel, toe heel. Iggy was sure she could do that and was about to join the end of the first line when she saw Daphne already there. Iggy didn't want to stand next to Daphne and felt Daphne was once again in her spot! Iggy grabbed her notebook but instead of writing, threw it down on the floor.

Immediately someone picked it up and Iggy reached out to take it back, when she heard the voice of her big sister Peony.

"Pink potatoes, something is not right," said Peony, and began opening the book.

"Don't," said Iggy trying to grab the book back.

But Peony held the book high and read what Iggy had written. A few moments later she said, "Your clues show lots of things going wrong. Want to talk about it?"

Iggy usually liked when Peony looked at her writing and explained what it showed. Only this time Iggy was too upset to talk. "Leave me alone," whispered Iggy, not wanting Ms. Tapiq to hear her and send her out of the room, maybe even out of the show. "And why are you here?"

Peony sat next to her and whispered, "My school had early dismissal so it was my chance to see you practice for your recital. Only you're not dancing. I can see why in your handwriting clues. Do you want me to explain?"

"No," said Iggy, feeling too upset to think.

Peony shrugged and said, "I suppose you're pink perfect and don't need to practice with everyone else."

"No, I'm not perfect," said Iggy feeling awful having to admit it. "I can't do the hop right but Daphne and Ms. Tapiq won't let me stand in the best spot to learn."

Peony nodded and asked, "Can I help?"

Iggy glanced at Daphne wishing she was dancing there instead, and said, "Do my handwriting clues show why I can't do the dance steps right?"

"Yes," said Peony pointing to the page and said very quietly, "If you will listen, I'll explain."

Iggy squeezed her hands together, took a deep breath, and nodded.

Peony moved closer to Iggy and began. "First let's look at the two names you wrote, Ms. Tapiq and Daphne. Writing names shows how you feel about those people. Are you ready to hear that?"

"They were both unfair to me," said Iggy trying hard to keep to a whisper.

"Yes, that is what you wrote, now let's see why you feel that way. Are your ears still listening?"

Iggy nodded and Peony pointed to the specific letters in Iggy's notebook as she spoke.

page 22
Ms. Tapiq is unfair
Daphne is unfair
Sitting quiet is unfair
I want to dance now!

Writing ↗*p* with a tall stem shows you are quick to argue. Sometimes you write a tall stem but usually your stem is short like this →*p* in the word page. Today you wrote your quick to argue tall stem *p* in both names *Tapiq* and *Daphne* which shows something happened that made you quick to argue with them both, is that right?"

Iggy nodded knowing it was true, and Peony continued, "Your usual *q* has a long leg *q*↙ showing you stick to things for a long time. But today your *q* in *Tapiq*↙ has a short leg which shows not spending your usual long time and giving up too soon. And because it's in Ms. Tapiq's name it means it has to do with Ms. Tapiq or tap class."

"But, I'm trying as hard as I can," Iggy argued, feeling sure she was right about that.

Peony nodded, "Yes, in your mind you are trying as hard as you can, but somehow it's not working and you gave up too soon. Is that right?"

Iggy wanted to scream but instead whispered, "I keep trying and I can't hop."

Peony nodded again and said, "I see why you can't get the dance steps right in your r. Peony pointed back to the paper and continued, "Your ↗〰 has points up on it for thinking. You naturally think about everything you do. But dance is different. Dance is based on smooth movements where stopping to think stops the smooth moves."

Peony stopped talking to write →ⁿ, then said, "People with a flat top r have natural smooth movement in their hands and feet. For dance you'll be better once you can just feel the moves instead of stopping to think about how the moves should go."

Iggy felt herself tighten like when she lost balance on the hop, and whispered through a choked voice, "I'm trying to figure out how to do the hop smoothly but it doesn't work."

Peony patted Iggy's arm and said, "You're used to figuring things out fast and doing it all by yourself. This will take a little more time and may need some help from others. Now this last clue is the one that might solve it. Are you still listening?"

Iggy nodded and Peony went on, "Last is the sharp point on top of your s ↙←. It shows you stick steadfast to your decisions and don't want to give in to what others suggest."

"Why should I give in?" asked Iggy, trying her hardest to keep to a whisper. "I just want to stand behind Ms. Tapiq where Daphne was so I can get the steps right. I have as much right to that spot as Daphne."

Peony tapped the ↙← and said, "Sometimes sticking with a decision doesn't help and sometimes others have good suggestions. If you use your thinking points, you can solve this problem by thinking of other ways to learn how to do the steps right. Do you want me to help you think of another way?"

Iggy shook her head no, wanting to think of another way by herself. She squeezed her hands together watching Daphne do a high hop and wished that was her. Then all at once she jumped up and announced, "I'm ready to try again!"

Iggy rushed to the end of the line next to Daphne and whispered, "My sister told me why I did what I did. I was quick to argue, I don't feel the dance steps, I gave up too fast, and I don't give in to suggestions. It was me who was unfair. I'm sorry." Iggy then put on her smile face and tried to hop the way Daphne did. But Iggy's feet just didn't do it right. She stood still watching Daphne and asked, "I can't get it, will you explain it to me?"

"It's easy," said Daphne placing her hand on her left leg. "After the left heel brush, raise your left knee super fast to lift you off the ground."

Iggy thought of Daphne's words. She was also thinking how much she wanted to make her parents, Peony, and Ms. Tapiq proud. For that she wouldn't give up too soon no matter how long it took. Iggy tried and tried to raise her left knee super fast to lift her off the ground. After many tries she began to feel the flow of the move without having to stop to think about it.

A minute later Daphne touched Iggy's arm and said, "You got it! You'll be great on stage."

"I did get it," said Iggy feeling proud of herself, though she knew it was because Peony explained why she did what she did, and Daphne explained to raise her knee super fast. Her thank you note to Peony would be,

Thank you for my
pyrs & pyrs clues!
☀ *Iggy* ☮

But there was no time to write a note to Daphne. Instead Iggy said, "Thank you for telling me the right way to hop, I couldn't figure it out. You're good at feeling the right moves to do."

"You're good at it now," said Daphne giving her a smile.

Iggy glanced towards Ms. Tapiq who noticed Iggy and turned to face her. Iggy's cheeks spread wide to show she was ready to smile for the audience and be on stage. Then Iggy did the hop, lifting herself off the ground with her super fast left knee. Ms. Tapiq gave her a pleased nod and Iggy felt so proud of herself. She couldn't wait for recital night. She would dance as best she could and smile as wide as she could to make the audience happy.

Iggy practiced lifting her knee super fast all the way out of tap class.

"You know what?" asked Iggy when she and Peony entered Mom's car.

"What?" asked both Peony and Mom together.

Iggy said in her most serious voice, "I know I was quick to argue, I gave up too fast, and I think better than I dance. But with a sister to explain it all and practicing a better dancer's smooth move suggestion, I learned to do the steps right. And you know why?"

"Why?" asked Peony and Mom at the same time once more.

"Because," said Iggy, bouncing up and down in her seat, "dancers know that the show must go on!"

6. tuv me

Iggy watched her 13 year old sister Peony scrub a pimple and wished she had a pimple to scrub. She liked doing what Peony did. But Iggy didn't have any pimples.

Peony complained to the bathroom mirror, "This pimple keeps getting bigger. When will it go away?"

Iggy didn't know any facts to tell about pimples. All she knew was Peony just spent 15 minutes looking in the mirror and she couldn't wait another second to ask her question for the third time that morning. She asked hopefully, "Now can you help me write my story?"

Peony wiped her face with a towel and said, "No, I have to work on my own story and can't waste any more time." Peony took one more look at her pimple then rushed out of the bathroom.

Iggy stood there feeling awful that Peony thought her story a waste of time. Peony didn't even think it worth the time spent on a pimple. Iggy felt so bad she yelled into the mirror, "My story is not a waste of time. My story will be better than hers and I'll be famous before she is. Then she'll be the one feeling bad!"

Iggy rushed to her room to write. Soon she had two sentences she was very proud of. She returned to the bathroom, looked into the mirror as if she was on TV, and said, "I, Iggy Pensky, will soon be a famous author for eight year olds like me. This is my story."

Iggy gave a quick cough, then continued in her most grown up voice, "Travel the universe to Pinkspot Planet where valuable messages hide in every pinkspot pimple. At first, some people feel they're ugly and try to scrub them away. But other people are quick to see that, staring them right in their face, are important messages they need to learn."

Peony suddenly appeared behind Iggy in the mirror and asked, "What are you doing?"

"Why do you want to know?" asked Iggy shutting her notebook.

Peony looked at the closed book and said, "Mom asked me to make sure you don't get in trouble while she's out shopping."

"I'm not in trouble," said Iggy gripping her book tighter. She was too mad to show Peony what she wrote and shouted, "Stop looking at my book and go away!"

"Temper, temper," said Peony shaking her head. "What are you writing that you don't want me to see?"

"None of your business," Iggy yelled.

"Don't you want my help?" asked Peony.

"Not anymore!" shouted Iggy. And with a sudden burst of anger, Iggy pushed her notebook into Peony's arm to make her leave. But before Iggy could pull the notebook back, Peony grabbed it and ran for her room. Iggy shouted after her, "That's not fair, give it back!"

But Peony didn't stop and when Iggy appeared inside Peony's room, Peony cried out, "Your title is Pinkspot Planet! You're the one not fair, you're stealing my story!"

"You're wrong," Iggy yelled back. "Pinkspot Planet is nothing like your Pinkadotsy Planet. You're mad because my story is better."

"Better? Pink impossible it's better," said Peony, pointing to 3 of Iggy's t's as she read, "Travel the universe to Pinkspot ↖ Planet ↖ where valuable messages hide in every pinkspot ↖ pimple."

Travel the universe to Pinkspot ↖ Planet ↖ where valuable messages hide in every pinkspot ↖ pimple.

Peony continued, "Look at your willful t-bars pushing your own personal goals onto others without caring how that feels to anyone else. A good writer needs to care about their characters' feelings to make their stories better. A writer who only cares about themselves does not make a story better."

Iggy knew she often didn't consider what other people felt. But Peony had no right to say Iggy's story could not be better than hers. She glared at Peony as she said, "My t-bars look strong and being strong is good."

"Good for your goal only," said Peony, "But too strong forces what you want on others and that's wrong."

"I'm not wrong," shouted Iggy. "My story is better than yours. If you think yours is better then you're wrong!"

Peony leaned back and asked, "Is your real goal to write better than me?"

"Yes!" shouted Iggy, feeling entitled to hurt Peony for calling her story a waste of time. "And I'll be a famous author before you."

Peony squeezed her hands together as she said, "Watch out for goals that push hurt on others, especially given your temper tics."

"Temper tics!" Iggy shrieked, "I don't have temper tics." She didn't know what temper tics were but she had felt teased when Peony said 'temper temper' and temper tics sounded worse.

"Then tell me what these are?" asked Peony pointing to the sharp angles at the beginning of the u and v.

→universe & →valuable

Iggy looked at them carefully seeing the sharp angles and insisted, "Those are not temper tics. They're points up for curious thinking, like in my m's."

Peony shook her head and said, "Points up curious thinking shows inside letters. A temper tic is a short sharp angle at the beginning of a letter that shows you get mad fast. In fact, your temper came fast just before when I asked what you were doing."

"It did not!" yelled Iggy. This was too much for her to take and she screamed, "Go away and leave me alone!"

Peony got quiet for a moment then said just above a whisper, "Pink fine, I'll go. I have better things to do than fight."

Peony turned away and left the room. Iggy wanted to shout after her to stay out, then realized she was left alone in Peony's room. Peony never left Iggy alone in her room. In fact, Iggy was yelled at if she went in there alone. And here she was left alone to do what she wanted. And what she wanted to do was make Peony feel as bad as Peony made her feel. Instantly she knew what would hurt Peony the most. She would read Peony's diary.

Iggy began looking for the small pink leather book. She looked on the dresser but it wasn't there. She looked under the pillow but it wasn't there, either. Next Iggy opened the closet and saw a bit of pink between the sweaters on the shelf. Iggy immediately took the book and read the first page written in pink print. Iggy was relieved because print was still easier for her to read. Peony knew that and printed the notes to Iggy that were extra important. Iggy wondered if this was one of those notes and read carefully...

PEONY'S DIARY

For my eyes only
Not because I'm mean
But for my eyes only
Because what I write belongs to me

If you think that's not fair
Instead of starting to yell
Ask me to explain what I write in here
And I will tell

Don't forget about others
And think you're always right
You know reading my diary is wrong
So please, let's not fight.

Iggy wanted to turn the page but the poem made her stop. Was this a test from Peony to her to see what she would do? Iggy wanted to pass the test right. She read the poem again and again. After the third time, even though it made her feel bad to admit it, she knew Peony's poem was right. Iggy returned the diary between the sweaters and went to where Peony sat writing in her Pinkadotsy Planet notebook.

Iggy stood in front of Peony's chair and asked, "What do you write in your diary?"

Peony closed her notebook and asked, "Did you read it?"

"Yes... no," said Iggy, "just the poem. I put it back between the sweaters. What you write belongs to you unless I ask, right?"

"Like the Pinkadotsy Planet story?" asked Peony. "Is that mine unless you ask?"

"That's different," said Iggy, "I used a different planet name and pimples on people instead of dots."

"It's still stealing my story of people with dots that give them messages, you just changed two words," said Peony hugging her notebook in her arms.

Iggy hadn't thought about it that way and said, "But I didn't mean to steal your story, it was because I think your story is so great that I want to be a great writer like you."

Peony looked at the floor for a moment, then back at Iggy and said, "I'm not a great writer, my first 3 chapters were rejected by 5 publishers. There's only one publisher who said they would look at it again if I make it better. That's what I write about in my diary. I feel too awful to tell anyone."

"Those five publishers are wrong," said Iggy, "your story is extra great. I can't wait to find out what happens!"

Peony half smiled and said, "Your opinion makes me feel better about my story, but I don't feel better you stole my story and pretended it's yours. That's wrong."

"What's wrong," began Iggy, feeling so upset at being told once more that she stole Peony's story, "is you thought I was a waste of your time, less important than a pimple!"

Peony shook her head and said, "Now that is pink wrong. It's having to spend so much time scrubbing my face that's a waste of my time. I like our time together and I learn a lot from you. But sometimes I have other things I must do, like the 3 chapters. The publisher wants it back in 2 days."

Iggy took in this new information and saw she really had been wrong. She prided herself on always having the right facts and right answers. Being wrong meant she had failed. She felt even worse than before and cried out, "How can it happen that I start out sure I'm right and end up all wrong?"

Peony pointed to Iggy's notebook and asked, "Do you want handwriting clues to show you why?"

Iggy thought of the bad sounding words willful and temper tics, and was scared to hear even more bad things about herself. But she had to understand how she had been wrong instead of right and never let it happen again. She asked, "Do you have the time to show me?"

"Pink yes," said Peony, "fighting is the biggest waste of time. Spending a few minutes to understand why we do what we do is a much better choice. Let's start with the t-bars."

"T-bars?" asked Iggy, immediately remembering Peony called hers willful. She was not sure she still wanted to hear about her clues.

Peony must have noticed Iggy turn away because she said, "A few of your t-bars are willful, but most are very impressive willpower. Are your ears open to listen?"

Iggy's worry was now curious to hear about her impressive willpower, which Peony made sound good. She nodded and Peony wrote numbers and arrows pointing to Iggy's t-bars.

1↗the universe

2↗to Pinkspot ↖3

Then Peony began, "The height of the t-bar shows how high a person sets their goals. Your t-bars are high on the stem which shows you set high goals that take a lot of hard work and a long time to reach. That by itself is very impressive about you."

Iggy realized she had been holding her breath, but now let it out at hearing her high t-bars were impressive. She listened closely as Peony went on.

"Also important is a t-bar's length and pressure. The length is how long your enthusiasm for your goal will last. How deep a dent the pen presses into the page is the force of your energy to get your goal done. The longer and deeper pressed the bar, the more willpower you have to reach your goal. Your willpower is very strong except when it goes too long and too heavily pressed, then it's…"

Iggy suddenly blurted it out herself, "Willful?"

Peony nodded and Iggy immediately had to ask, "How bad is my willful?"

"Not really bad," said Peony. "You just haven't had a reason to think about it before. A willful person pushes their goal on others without concern for other people's goals. They believe their goal is the only one that matters."

"And I do that?" asked Iggy.

"Sometimes," said Peony, "but only sometimes. It's only in some of your t-bars. Do you see it in #3?"

1↗ *the universe*

2↗ *to Pinkspot* ↖3

Iggy saw her willful t-bar was very long and grew thicker. The word pushy jumped in her head and she asked, "That t-bar looks pushy like my g, j and q. Does that mean I could push someone when I want to do my goal?"

"Pink impressive you are as always," said Peony. "The push in your g, j and q start below the baseline in the leg action zone. *l y r F q l* . Those pushes show you could physically push someone if you get mad enough."

Iggy had heard that from Peony before and said, "You told me that if I stop to think I could stop from pushing someone."

"Pink right," said Peony. "This push is different because it's not in the leg action zone. Your t-bar push is in your head thinking zone."

Iggy looked from her legs area for physical action *l y r F q l* to her t-bar in the head thinking zone. She knew both had strong push but was still confused. She asked, "Is willful when it's a person's thinking in their head that is pushy, meaning all they think about is pushing their goals to make them happen but their thinking doesn't think about what happens to anyone else?"

Peony laughed and said, "Your thinking on that is pink get-to-the-point perfect!"

"And I do that?" asked Iggy feeling scared about what Peony would say.

Peony immediately said, "Not usually. Mostly your t-bars are willpower. You just have to be aware that you can beome willful sometimes. Knowing about it helps you recognize when it happens."

Iggy touched her strong willpower t-bars t then her pushy willful t-bar t and asked, "Can I make a goal to stick to strong willpower and not let it get pushy?"

"Pink petunia yes," said Peony smiling but tightened her lips as she said, "but it won't be easy for you to stick to that when your temper gets mad. Look at your u & v."

Peony pointed to

→*universe* & →*valuable*

and continued, "Both those letters begin with sharp angle temper tics that show you can get mad fast. Ms. Loops says an angry person wants others to feel as bad as they feel until they understand the whole situation that made them feel bad."

"That happened to me," said Iggy now understanding how that made her thinking go wrong. "But once I understood you didn't think my story was a waste of time but you needed your time to write for the publisher, I stopped being mad and realized what was right." Iggy looked back at her writing and asked, "Can I use my willpower on that, too?"

"Pink yes," said Peony, "but there's one more clue I want you to see. Let's look at your natural reactions. Do you see the bottom on your u v in valuable?

Iggy went from feeling great about her willpower to upset that she had done something else wrong. She said, "I see I wrote that u wrong. It should be rounder on the bottom."

"It's not wrong for you," said Peony. "Narrow bottoms with v-shape sides like on both of your u's, ᴜ & ᴜ, show you have a narrow reaction time and are fast to say what's on your mind. Wider bottoms like I write on my ᴜ shows I have a wider reaction time to consider what I feel and how others feel before I say anything."

Iggy always liked hearing about her fast reactions and was proud of the fast thinking bottom angles in her ᴜ's. But these fast reactions had her confused. She asked, "Are narrow bottom u's good or bad?"

Peony smiled and said, "Use your fast reactions to figure this out. Is fast reaction to say what's on your mind good when a person is mad?"

Iggy immediately got the point and said excitedly, "No, it's better to have a wider or longer reaction time when you're mad."

"Pink correct said Peony. "That's one more use for your impressive willpower. Use it to slow down your mad reaction until you take time to think. Will you set one of your goals to do that?"

"Yes!" Iggy shouted, "I'm setting my willpower on controlling my temper tics, my willful t-bars, and my fast to speak reactions when I'm mad. It's lucky I have a lot of strong willpower because I'll need it!"

Peony laughed, then waved her pen in the air like a wand and said, "I now give you two pinkadotsy messages."

Peony drew two circle dots on Iggy's arm and said, "Pinkadotsy Message #1 is the most important message for you. It is beware of getting mad fast."

"I'll beware," said Iggy frowning at that dot, "getting mad makes my thinking go wrong."

"Pink true for everyone," said Peony, then pointed to the other dot, "And Pinkadotsy Message #2 holds these 3 magic words to use whenever someone makes you feel bad. They are, 'Is something wrong?'"

Iggy sat up straight and sang in a deep voice, "Is something wrong?"

"Pink perfect performance!" said Peony smiling wide. "Asking 'Is something wrong?' clears up misunderstandings and shows you what's right."

Iggy jumped up and down saying, "Asking what is wrong shows you what's right," then stopped to say, "I just had a new idea for my story. It has a pimple message like your dots, but I won't write it or tell it to anyone but you. Is that still wrong?"

"Just for me is pink fine," said Peony leaning back in her chair and added, "my ears are wide open."

Iggy stood in front of Peony and said, "Once upon a time there was a pimple that wouldn't go away no matter how hard the girl scrubbed. One day the pimple said, 'Your scrubbing is not a waste of time. I will go away but first I am a reminder that hard work, like all that scrubbing, can make wrong things go away. Like if you keep working hard at writing, the publisher's wrong replies will go away and their letters will say your story is exactly right. And when your little sister does wrong things, if you keep working hard to help her understand why she's wrong, her wrong will go away and she will begin doing what's right.' The girl thanked her pimple for being an important reminder and never called scrubbing a pimple a waste of her time again."

Peony clapped and said, "You could be a famous writer some day."

"If I keep willpower over willful," said Iggy, feeling extra great to hear that from Peony, but also feeling another idea pushing to come out of her mouth. "Do you want to hear the part 2?"

"Pink sure," said Peony leaning back again to wait.

Iggy twirled herself in a circle then began, "The girl thought of her pimple message that hard work can turn what's wrong into what's right. She wanted to give that message to her little sister in a way she'd never forget. She drew a pink dot on little sister's arm with a wide bottom smile next to it. Big sister then announced, 'The dot holds your beware of getting mad fast message, the smile holds your solution. With hard work you can make what goes wrong for you turn into what goes right.' Little Sister looked at her messages, knowing it was important to take the time to consider their possibilities. She then felt her short bottom frown spread into a wide bottom smile. With it she felt her quick angry reactions give her willpower time to slowly consider and react. Little sister then declared, 'Smiles widen the way for willpower to work!' Iggy spread her arms wide and said, "That's the story's end and the beginning of little sister's messages to remember."

Peony immediately stood and wrapped her arms around Iggy in a big hug, then said, "You wrote your messages exactly right for you. I now have to change my mind. You already are a great writer!"

"I'm a great writer like you!" said Iggy, her big smile growing bigger. Right now she was happy to stand still and let Peony hug her. Except her mind quickly jumped into thinking of a letter she would write to the publisher about Peony's Pinkadotsy Planet story, saying, 'This story of pink dots on people's skin giving them the messages they need is as great as people's own handwriting giving them the messages they need.'

"You know what?" asked Iggy.

"What?" asked Peony.

"Your handwriting clues are the best messages I could ever get," said Iggy, "Even when I'm famous I'll remind myself to take time to figure out what's right because you took the time to explain my *two* messages to me."

7. wxyz me

Iggy looked at the snow falling outside and shouted, "It's not fair! Today I'm 9 and no one can come to my birthday party."

Iggy's 13 year old sister Peony said, "Lizzy next door is coming. That's why I'm drawing this big iguana."

"I don't want Lizzy," said Iggy, slumping in a chair next to Peony. "She never wants to do anything I want to do. I want my party tomorrow."

Peony put down the green marker and said, "Tomorrow we travel to Grandma's for winter break. Then you have birthday parties to attend the two weekends after that. Mom says it has to be today."

"But," said Iggy, "I want a real birthday party with lots of kids and lots of presents."

"You have presents," said Peony, "from Mom & Dad and our grandparents. You'll get Lizzy's present soon and mine at 6:30 tonight, the time you were born."

Iggy slapped her hands on the table and said, "It's not fair to wait till 6:30, I want it now!"

Peony tightened her lips and said, "You'll wait and not complain or I'll rip it up. It's a time for willpower over temper tics, remember?"

Iggy remembered Peony's pinkadotsy message to beware of getting mad fast and her own added wide-bottom smile to widen her time to react. She also knew to stop arguing when Peony's lips went tight. If she didn't, Peony would not talk to her for days. And even worse, Peony would rip her present.

The doorbell rang and Peony said, "You get it, I have to finish drawing this iguana before the party."

Iggy almost argued that only having Lizzy was not a party but thought of Peony's warnings. She put her hand over her mouth to keep from speaking too fast before thinking, and went to the door.

Lizzy stood there covered in snow. She held out a box wrapped in shiny green paper, and said, "Happy Birthday Iggy, this is for you."

Iggy smiled at the gift and opened it while they walked inside to where Peony sat. "Thanks," said Iggy, shaking out the plastic reptiles from the box. "Let's see, an alligator, turtle, gecko, rattlesnake, and lizard."

"That's not a lizard," said Lizzy dropping her snowy jacket on the floor, "it's an iguana, for your iguana-theme birthday party."

Iggy held up the green lizard in front of Lizzy to point out the obvious mistake and said, "I know iguanas are a kind of lizard, but do you see the iguana third eye on top of its head?"

Lizzy crossed her arms in front of her and said, "My name is not Iguana like yours, and I don't know iguana stuff like you do."

Iggy nodded and said, "Of course your name's not Iguana, but it's Lizzy for Lizard."

Lizzy laughed and said, "You're silly, Lizzy is for Elizabeth. Didn't you know that?"

Since last month when Lizzy moved next door, Iggy thought Lizzy stood for Lizard. It was the only thing she liked about Lizzy, that they both had reptile names. Iggy was upset she had been wrong and said, "Lizzy for Lizard is better. Lizards can break off their tail if they get caught in a trap and grow a new one. Wouldn't you like to be able to do that?"

"No," said Lizzy. "I don't have a tail to get caught in a trap. Do you?"

"Yes," said Iggy, holding up one of the tails Peony cut from green paper for tape-the-tail-on-the-iguana. "And I have a third eye." She popped a black paper circle on top of her head for tape-the-third-eye-on-the-iguana and said, "I can see everywhere, no one can sneak up on me."

"You're silly," said Lizzy, "People don't have a third eye, ask Peony."

They both stared at Peony who just finished drawing the iguana.

"That's where the third eye goes," said Iggy pointing to the black spot on top of the iguana's head.

Lizzy looked at the black spot, then at Peony and asked, "People don't have a third eye, right?"

"Actually," said Peony, "My Handwriting Clues Club teacher, Ms. Loops, says handwriting is our third eye.

Our two eyes see what's outside of us. Handwriting is a third eye to see what's inside of us."

"That's silly," said Lizzy.

"No it's not," said Iggy. "Peony, show her."

Peony taped the iguana picture to the wall, pointed to the tails on the table, and said, "Let's play tape-the-tail-on-the-iguana."

"No," said Iggy, "show her how the third eye works."

Peony turned to Lizzy and asked, "What do you want to do?"

Lizzy sat on a chair at the table and said, "I don't feel like tape-the-tail-on-a-silly-iguana. I guess show me the third eye."

"Okay," said Peony, placing a sheet of paper in front of Lizzy and asked, "Do you like to write?"

Lizzy smiled and said, "I love to write. My mom has me practice cursive every day."

Iggy sat next to Lizzy in front of another blank page, and said, "I practice cursive every day, too."

"Two cursive writing girls together, this is pink great," said Peony.

Iggy wished Peony had said Iggy's handwriting is pink great. Iggy decided to say it for her and stated, "Peony says I write better than half her class."

"I write neater than my big brother and his friends," said Lizzy.

"Good for you both," said Peony, handing each of them a pen, "Now write the alphabet a to z in cursive."

Iggy wrote fast. She loved writing fast with her pen feeling like it was sliding on whipped cream, the way Peony told her it would feel if she practiced. When she finished she looked at Lizzy who was still writing. Iggy felt proud she was faster than Lizzy but she did wish Lizzy would hurry up because she didn't like to wait.

Soon Lizzy was done and Peony put the two alphabets next to each other. Iggy wanted Peony to say, 'Oh, Iggy, your writing is so much better than Lizzy's.' But what Peony said was, "Will you look at that, we have both strong and light pressure here today. This will be most interesting."

Iggy thought hers looked like the strong one and said, "I'm stronger than Lizzy. I carry my book bag while Lizzy needs wheels on hers."

"Both book bags get to school the best way for each of you," said Peony with a smile.

Iggy was disappointed Peony didn't call her stronger and asked, "Are you looking at my strong t-bars?"

"Actually," said Peony, "I'm looking at the letters wxyz. The last thing people write is their most natural writing. Are you both ready to hear what the third eye sees?"

"Ready," shouted Iggy. Lizzy also said she was ready, though in a much softer voice. Iggy was sure her louder voice was better.

Peony placed the two alphabets on the table and covered all the letters except the last four.

wxyz   *wxyz*

"Let's look at the w," said Peony. "My third eye sees two important clues for how you both are on the inside when it comes to playing games. Iggy's w has pointy angle bottoms which shows she is competitive and plays to win."

Peony switched to Lizzy's writing and said, "Lizzy's *w* has curvy round bottoms which shows she cares more about having fun than winning. Both w's are perfectly fine, they just show how different you each are on the inside."

"It's better to win," said Iggy. She couldn't possibly think of not wanting to win.

"Not to everyone," said Peony, "and having fun is as good a reason to play games as winning. Now let's look at the x's."

wxyz   *wxyz*

Peony pointed to each x and said, "My third eye is looking at your x lines. The biggest difference is the pressure. Iggy's *x* lines press deep on the paper which she knows shows she has a good memory, but also shows she has lots of energy and needs lots of physical activity."

Peony moved her finger and said, "Lizzy's *x* has light lines from her soft press on the paper which shows she has a small amount of energy, gets tired easily and needs a lot of sitting activities."

Iggy saw her deeply pressed lines compared to Lizzy's light lines and said, "I have so much energy I can do a hundred jumping jacks and not get tired."

Lizzy shrugged and said, "You jumped around so much in my room you broke my night light."

"It was an accident and I said I'm sorry," argued Iggy.

Peony looked sympathetic and said, "Knowing your different energy levels helps understand each other better. Do you want to hear more from the third eye?"

"Yes," said Iggy loudly while Lizzy sat back and gave a short nod.

Peony pointed to the y's and said, "Here the third eye sees both long and short legs."

They all looked at both y legs y and y.

Peony went on, "Iggy's long leg shows she naturally sticks with activities for a long time till they're done. Lizzy's short leg shows she naturally only sticks with activities for a short time before she wants to stop."

"I spend all day making up trivia games," said Iggy, "Can Lizzy do that?"

"Lizzy is different than you," said Peony. "She gets bored fast, then wants to do something else."

"That's right," said Lizzy, "and I'm bored now."

"Do you want to hear the z clue?" asked Peony. "It's the most interesting one."

"Yes," said Iggy, bouncing up and down in her seat.

Lizzy just shrugged and Peony knew Lizzy was ready to stop. She spoke quickly while she still had Lizzy's attention.

They all looked at *z* and *z*.

Then Peony said in a high squeaky voice, "Your z's are the biggest surprise of all!"

Lizzy giggled and Peony continued in her regular voice, "Believe it or not, you both have the same clue. The narrow loops on both your z's show you both only want to do what you already like and not try something new."

"Of course I only want to do what I already like," said Iggy.

"Me, too," said Lizzy.

Peony laughed, "See how alike you two are? Now decide what to do next."

Iggy immediately said, "I want to do the iguana trivia test."

"Not me," said Lizzy standing up and heading for her coat. "I don't know the answers and I'm going home."

"Wait," said Peony to Lizzy, "let the third eye tell us what you can do together that you will both like."

Lizzy stopped to listen and Peony lined up the letters

wxyz   wxyz

Peony pointed to the w's and began. "Lizzy's curvy w tells us it has to be just for fun for Lizzy even though Iggy's pointy w likes to win.

Peony pointed to the x's and said, "Lizzy's light press shows she needs time to rest while Iggy's deep press shows she needs physical activity.

Peony tapped the y's and said, "And Lizzy's short leg y shows if she gets bored she wants to stop while Iggy's long y likes to keep on doing for a long time. So putting these 3 clues together, here's an idea. You ready to hear it?"

Iggy and Lizzy both nodded and Peony was excited she was almost there.

Peony continued, "If it's just for fun, and if Iggy acts out the iguana facts while Lizzy watches from the couch, and if Iggy stops and does something else if Lizzy gets bored, will you both do it?"

"I will," shouted Iggy, excited for a chance to talk about iguanas and especially to act like one.

"Okay," said Lizzy, happy to get to sit on the couch.

Iggy stood in the middle of the room as if on a big stage and did her best iguana imitations. She demonstrated how iguanas stick their tongues out to eat bugs. She jumped on the couch to show how iguanas grip their feet onto branches. She bumped her back into the wall, pretending her tail was stuck in a trap and she had to break it off. Iggy tried to make each trivia fact funnier than the one before, and Lizzy laughed louder each time. Iggy was thrilled with Lizzy's laughs and wanted to keep her laughing more.

For the last fact, Iggy decided to show how iguanas use their tail as a weapon. She stuck out her butt and shook it pretending it was a sword. Lizzy laughed so hard she started kicking her legs in the air. Iggy began swinging her arms in the air like a sword fight between two tails. Then they both laughed so hard they had to stop laughing to catch their breaths.

Lizzy soon calmed down enough to say, "This might be silly but I like making flash cards. Maybe we can write third eye trivia flash cards and put them in a space capsule for three eyed aliens to find in the future?"

"Great idea," said Iggy, "Let's do it."

Lizzy picked up a pen and said, "You say the facts and I'll write."

Iggy jumped up and down and said, "Fact #1, Third eyes see shadows and light."

Iggy jumped more until Lizzy finished writing, then said, "Fact #2, Third eyes alert iguanas to danger from above and behind."

Lizzy wrote and then said, "I have Fact #3, Iggy and Lizzy only need two eyes in their head because handwriting is their third eye."

Both girls laughed and Lizzy said, "I'll draw a different color third eye for every fact you say."

Iggy had 7 more facts and they were so busy it was a surprise when Iggy's mom & dad walked in with the birthday cake. Iggy and Lizzy ate while making up names for three eyed aliens like Icing Eyes and Chocolate Peepers. And they were both surprised when it was 6 o'clock and time for Lizzy to go home.

"So soon?" asked Iggy, not wanting Lizzy to leave. Lizzy yawned and said, "I am tired but this was the most fun Iguana party I've ever been to. Maybe you can do lizard trivia at my birthday party?"

"Yes," shouted Iggy excited for the chance to act like a lizard. But then, watching Lizzy leave, she felt bad her party was over.

Iggy saw Peony sit down to write in her notebook. She knew Peony didn't like to be disturbed when she worked on her Pinkadotsy Planet story, but a half hour felt impossible to wait. Iggy asked, "Can I get your present now?"

Peony looked up and said, "The many angles in your writing show you don't like to wait. But they also show you like to win. Here's your contest. Wait 30 minutes and a pink great present will be your prize."

Iggy still didn't like waiting for 30 whole minutes but she did like contests and wanted to win. She sat on the floor right next to the reptiles then noticed their shapes. She decided to make up her own contest of which reptile had the most angles. They all had sharp angled teeth, but then she noticed they all had round parts, too.

She thought of Lizzy's writing *wxyz* with mostly round curves and how she smiled a lot. Lizzy was fun once they found something they both liked to do. Iggy wished Lizzy was still there and decided to have a contest to see which reptile had the best round part.

She picked up the turtle and said, "You have a round cereal bowl shell." She picked up the rattlesnake and said, "You have a round rope body." She picked up the alligator and said, "You have round jelly bean eyes." She picked up the gecko and said, "You have round mini-marshmallow toes. Last of all, she picked up the lizard and said, "You have a round u face like the shape of a smile. She decided that lizard was the winner because it had a smile like Lizzy's.

"6:30," called Peony holding out a large pink envelope with cursive writing on it that said,

Happy Birthday Iggy!

Iggy quickly opened the envelope and pulled out a green handmade book filled with samples of Iggy's writing and what the clues in each letter meant. Iggy pointed with excitement at the title,

Handwriting Clues Book
Iggy A-Z

then read the first page of Peony's written cursive out loud...

Your cursive clues are a present
You have learned to see
They are not only a present to you
But understanding you better is a present to me
This alphabet here is how you work inside
That shows so much greatness in you
And with all we'll continue to learn from each other
Together there is so much greatness we surely will do

I love you pink much!
Peony

Iggy held up the book and shouted, "This is the best present ever!" She rushed to Peony and gave her a big hug.

Peony hugged her back with delight, then said, "When you were born and came home from the hospital, Mom said to me, "This little sister is the greatest present you will ever get. And you know what?"

Iggy looked up in Peony's eyes and asked, "What?"

Peony shouted, "Mom was right!"

"I remember saying that," said Mom, "but I didn't know then how smart a present she would become. And speaking of presents, I'm sorry the snow made it a small party with only Lizzy's present for you."

Iggy stopped to think about that and said, "Small didn't matter, I had great big fun. You want to know why?"

"Why?" asked Mom, Dad & Peony at the same time.

Iggy announced, "Because of Peony's third eye clues, I found out Lizzy is a fun friend and it was my best party ever. And you know what else?"

"What?" they all asked together.

Iggy felt great excitement as she declared, "In the contest for what will make this my greatest year ever, learning more handwriting clues from Peony and being able to attend the Handwriting Clues Club will be this year's biggest winners!"

www.ingramcontent.com/pod-product-compliance
Lightning Source LLC
Chambersburg PA
CBHW041228270326
41935CB00002B/6